Mystical Musings of a Landlocked Mermaid

Mystical Musings of a Landlocked Mermaid

Creative Commons Copyright 2019

Donna J. Kelley

All rights reserved

Illustrations by Chris Parker @

https://www.deviantart.com/queenslandchris

And trulyonetoo @ https://www.deviantart.com/trulyonetoo

ISBN 978-0-359-96232-7

About the Author:

Donna Kelley is an upper New York state based poet, photographer, and author of the new book *Mystical Musings of a Landlocked Mermaid*. An avid photographer, she has spent over two decades writing poetry filled with vibrant images giving her poems their lush, picturesque quality. Her premiere collection is a reflection of her creativity and passion for writing and life. Donna has a BS in history from PSU where she received a History research project writing award and took numerous courses in creative writing. A number of her poems are featured on the Deviant Art website where she has collaborated with other artists to create unique pieces. Donna lives and works out of her home in the city of Plattsburgh in the heart of the Adirondacks and goes for long walks in nature whenever she has the chance. She is quite a genealogy nerd and collector of rocks and minerals as well as a huge fan of zombies and the paranormal.

Creation's Portrait

Golden beams of effervescent light,
sparkle and dance
like iridescent will-o-the wisp
cavorting on the serene
ultramarine loch.
Illuminating the
Prussian blue
aquatic depths
with voltaically charged,
waltzing sprites
of luminosity.
Spraying forth as glowing
chimera, from the depths,
in opalescent foam.
Dissipating at last in a
flamboyant jig of

```
                B       S
       U                E
   B       B
                   L
```

"The Bottle" CP

Message in a Bottle

Wistful wishes on a star
Memories of a little piece of heaven
Bodies tangled in bedclothes
Sweet salty and sensuous lips, tantalizing tongues intertwined.
Clasped hearts and hands, always and forever, until death do us part
Summer love.
.
Romantic notions
Written on a scrolled paper
Placed in a bottle, tossed into the sea
No return to sender.

Glistening in the water a buoyant bottle
Carrying an urgent message to anonymous
Bobs positively
Joyfully, on blue green waves.

Decades later….

Cold fingers fumble with a weathered cap
Pulling the contents out
Eyes glaze over while absorbing the message
Dreaming of a long lost love

"If people are meant to be,
they will always find their way back.
Crossing paths with you was something I'll be forever thankful for.
If we find each other again, I hope you never let this go.

This isn't our stories end, go be you and I'll be here when you get back.
Loving you was a little piece of heaven.
With All My Love."

Warmed fingers put the cap back in place
sentimental sentiments sealed in a glass tomb
shoved into a dark pocket
to be pulled out on a melancholy day
its sender conjured up, like a
spirit contacted by a ouija board.

Serendipitous Encounter

Warm summer breezes waft gleefully and gallantly through the gloaming,
as they carry an elegant ebony butterfly
fluttering her fairy like wings,
lithely toward fragrant meadows.
Cold hard metal.
Life interrupted.
The fragile form falls.
Darkness descends. Seconds, minutes and hours slip by and then,
the tiny, tattered body is gently picked up and cradled in the warmth of a human hand.
The lady flutters her wings, flying again as if in a dream,
while rocking back and forth in the curve
of a cocoon.
Her feet begin to move as if they are recalling memories of their own
Shapes, colors, sounds and smells run together muted, like a Monet painting.
Memories fall, echoing through time and darkness.
The sweet smell of nectar calls her back from the abyss.
She feels warmth surrounding her as she is lifted up to the edge of a flower
She sips the sweet syrup, moves her legs and flutters her wings
This must be heaven, she lets her thoughts drift and gives into the darkness, and dreams.
Miles away an old woman lies in the street, the warm summer wind wafting through her hair…

"Distant Shore" CP

Landlocked Mermaid

Blue green scintillating memories of
Glittering serpentine scales gliding gracefully
Weightlessly, beautifully buoyant
Through the sea, while
Bountiful tresses floating effortlessly on the water, like seaweed
they are but distant recollections bubbling and bobbing across the surface
Memories get stuck between gray rocky crevices
Shriveling and morphing into
Foreign appendages
Easily weighing down,
Woefully imprisoning
The once lithe enchantress

Pain is Beautiful

There is beauty in pain, sometimes…
when it lovingly focuses on
the tiniest details
as it paints with an icy crystalline precision point
on nerve endings
traveling through the nervous system like frost on a
window pane
It pauses poetically at times lulling its victim into a trance
before it takes up its palette again
painting a prettily poignant and searing
landscape brandishing broad strokes,
leaving its prey,
out of breath
weary
wishing for respite
perhaps even
a beautiful death

Fishbowl Fantasy

Come one, come all to
stare, stroke and salivate over this
delectable slice of meat
breasts, legs, rump- men
come join in the sinfully delicious
finger licking, delightful feast of flesh
never too much, never enough
for one
 watch her attempts to avoid
your gaze
look as she slinks by slowly
brazenly unaware
wares artfully arranged to
whet your appetite
exhibiting, tantalizing, titillating, protesting advances,
yet shamefully, no shamelessly
succumbing to your lascivious longings at last.

Bedtime Story

Pretty poppies placidly pontificate
Pacifying lullabies
Nodding heads
Breathe intoxicatingly synthesizing
Ambivalence
Sleep slowly spreads her dark cloak
Floating, falling, through the rabbit hole
Reach out, grab the pretty potion
Drink deeply
To forget, remember
Eat cake and grow
Strong
Break the glistening glass

It's an emergency!

White Lives Matter!!!

Circa 1492, Europeans sailed the ocean blue,
searching for
new land
A new beginning, new opportunities
the golden ticket, because
White lives matter!

Explorers leap from ships
leaving indelible boot prints on virgin soils
Seeking coveted riches,
Millions of indigenous cut down in their wake
like trees in a forest
clearing the landscape for
Blood tainted, manifest destiny dreams, because
White lives matter!

Boats arrive with African slave chattel
bought to tend plantations, but
treated like cattle.
Separated from families- beaten, bound, raped, and
branded, because
White lives matter!

White founding fathers,
slave owners, crafted the
Declaration of Independence and The Constitution
Built a great nation on
the whipped backs of the oppressed
Just so all property holding white men could be free to
pursue their dreams, because

White lives matter!

Imperialism's wet dreams of western expansion
Cross imaginary political borders,
It is their divine right
Slaying and raping, inferior brown skinned people, because
White lives matter!

White lives matter!

Segregation, sterilization, miscegenation, appropriation
No reparations.
Committed in the name of the sanctity of our nation, because
White lives matter!

Sparks ignite
Black individuals unite
And still they rise, like Maya Angelou's prophetic words,
so their voices may be heard, because
White lives have always mattered!!!
more than black lives.
The bells toll so,
all of the world may know
Black Lives Matter!!! just as much as white lives.

"Red" CP

Euphoric Intoxication

Dreamy divine diva ruffles border
the curvy bottom of a bodacious,bountiful
chocolate cupcake; while a
creamy cocoa ganache glaze coiffure perches perkily atop
moist mouthwatering, delectable decadence and
glittering gems of sugar sparkle sexily, tantalizing tingling
tongues.

Lime Seductress

Silky smooth, sweet and savory lines
boldly beckon
While luscious lemon lime essence
permeates senses
lingers lightly on lips
Languidly luscious and salty licks
coyly combine
creating a wildly wicked and
delicious margarita.

Rococo Merengue

Marie Antoinette meringue curls
piled to dizzyingly dangerous heights,
poise prettily and precariously atop a
magnificently moist
deliciously dense
decadently delightful cake.
Pink shimmering crystals cling tightly to every curve
of the fanciful frivolous icing.
like Mademoiselle Antoinette's corset,
they accentuate the shape of what lies beneath.
Unbridled Rococo merriment eagerly balances on silver
tines,
quivering in anticipation
of sweet pink lip's touch and the
tantalizingly seductive swirl of a warm tongue's, first taste.

"Memories" CP

Mangolicious

Tropical amber droplets glisten
while balancing delicately on
cinnamon red petals
dripping and trailing down decadent delicious dewy skin
rivulets revel in curves as they nonchalantly travel
toward tantalizing, tempting
unexplored territory
while salty sweet sensuous kisses eagerly
await the fruity essence

Slow Tease

Compelling creative conversations
act as an amorous aphrodisiac
when warm winsome words drip from luscious lips
creating puddles of
smoldering images in our minds.
lush lace like layers peeled away one by one
give glimpses of what lies beneath
intense tawdry teasing leads us by the hand to
the sensuous scintillescent sea of desire
building a perfect storm of tumultuous waves.
crashing in
leaving us helpless
to resist
as we lay spent, overcome by orgasmic emotion.

Dimpled Delightfully

A curtain of curls cascades,
sinfully sumptuous tendrils, fragrantly frame
dimpled, delightful, deliciously cool 'n creamy alabaster
orbs
Poised prettily on the precipice of sweet sensuous rapture
They hover in a cusp like arch over the radiating warmth
emanating from a moist crescent embrace
Tingling in anticipation, euphorically enveloped,
they eagerly await the branding of hot hard pearls
sinking ever so slowly, ecstatically reveling, in their
jubilant juiciness

Bodacious Brunette Locks

My curly, curvaceous tresses
languidly long,
lusciously lust
for
the tender touch
simmering with sensuality
lying burgeoning within your fingertips.
Anticipation rises to a crescendo, reminiscent
of the orgasmic vibration that courses throughout their
wanton   strands.
Like a heat seeking covetous missile, they searches for the
warmth and desire your hands
emanate.

Soul Mates

Momentarily mesmerized
mysteriously merged
enchanting enigmatic eyes emanate electrical pulses,
dancing delightfully as
deja vu casually conducts
rose-red, romantic, rhythmic, rumbas with
hot honeyed decadent delicious symphonies and
tangy tangerine tangos tremulously tempt, torture, titillate while
butterflies flutter frantic passionate purple palpitations in
proximity of promises with scorching spicy sonnets laced with
wicked whirlwinds of devilishly dewy luscious lips
lingering lithely, sensually showering secret
spaces delving deeply lavishing lilies lovingly, folds fondly
seeking, salmon stamens
mutually, mingling, mirroring,
sweetly sipping nectarine nectar

Contact

Sweet sensuous sentiments and sighs
whispered through cyber phone lines
from our lips to each other's fingertips
seduce, titillate and tease brain cells
coaxing cataclysmic climaxes
until lust spills over
in a flood of cream

"Gold Coast Moon" CP

Fate

Turn the corner and your whole world changes
A simple greeting
Hey, how are you liking the weather today?
Turns into hours long soliloquies
Pregnant with hopeful, hidden messages
friendly flirtatious phrases
Hours turn into days, months into years
Who knew a stranger would one day become someone
I love so dear?

Getting to Know You

Let's get down to the matter
the pink and gray squishy substance you store so secretly
And preciously,under
that seemingly durable dome.
Saw, probe and scalpel in hand
I delve in, detached, not fearing what awaits
skull fragments, neatly folded accordion layers of tissue
and blood give way.
Unscathed, I plunge in
squeezing your thoughts, memories and emotions in my
hands, letting them
ooze like slime through my fingers.
I taste your essence as I
bite into the core of your rubbery brain, stripping and
sucking the subsistence out
of the fragile exterior membrane, like
the hidden meat in a shrimp's tail,
I digest your pith
in the hope, I will get to know you better.

Homecoming

My mind wanders to you
as I wait
watching snowflakes drift gently, like feathers
to the ground.
I conjure up
Your beautiful brown eyes crinkle as warm laughter
escapes your lips
they soften as they gaze into mine,
just before you bend down and your sweet lips part to
meet mine
My heart skips a beat and my body tingles in anticipation
Feeling your hand caress my face.
The snowflakes are starting to dissipate
You are here at last and I am
Home.

Loving You

My mind wanders to you
as I wait
watching snowflakes drift gently, like feathers
to the ground.
I conjure up
Your beautiful brown eyes crinkle as warm laughter
escapes your lips
they soften as they gaze into mine,
just before you bend down and your sweet lips part to
meet mine
My heart skips a beat and my body tingles in anticipation
Feeling your hand caress my face.
The snowflakes are starting to dissipate
You are here at last and I am
Home.

More

Never enough time or
tender kisses
Long embraces and
laughter
clasped hands or
soulful gazing
clandestine meetings and
never Enough
Me and you

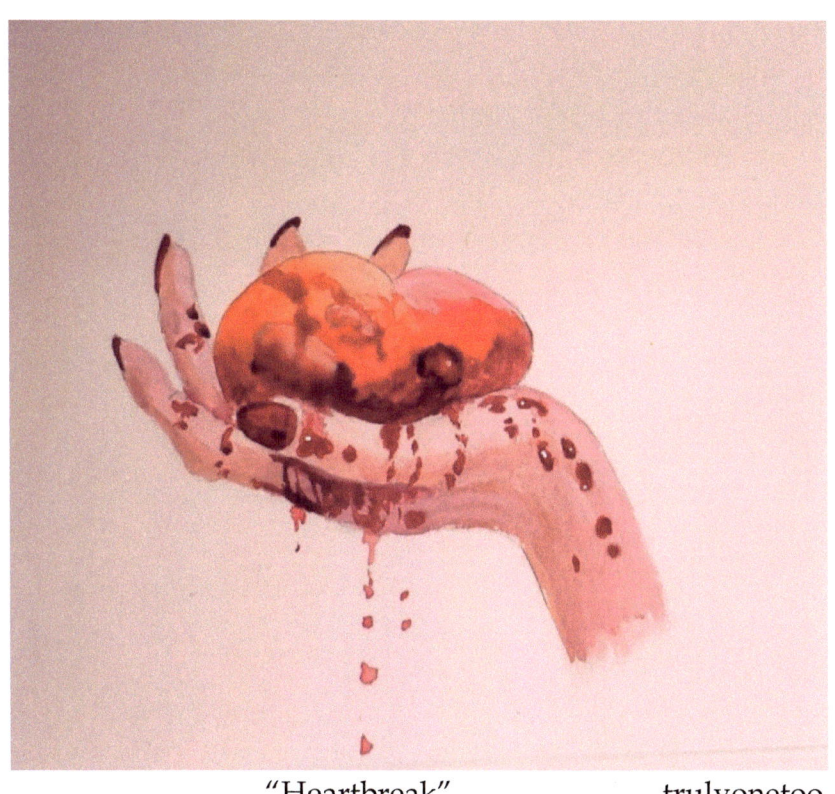

"Heartbreak" trulyonetoo

Heartbreak

Heart torn apart; lying in a sad state of disrepair.
It's lustrous interior exposes shrapnel of us ;
woven brazenly into its succulent scarlet secrecy.
Unbelievably,
its warm, bleeding, beating mass lies
naked in my trembling hands.
Its vermilion gushing vitality, beckons my
pearly white teeth
to sink into the throes of its anguish and feel its meaty
desolation,
the brine of its sorrow, between my teeth.

Without You

Grief steadily stalks, abruptly,
lustily, latches on
eager to fanatically feast
slowly sinking its razor sharp teeth
poignantly piercing, sweetly savoring sumptuous flesh,
greedily gustily
gluttonous,
carefully, consciously consuming.

With a horrifically heinous, macabre grin
voraciously vampiric
it sucks out joy jubilantly
licks its fingers feverishly
toying, twisting, tormenting and torturing
its lips and teeth stained blood red with meaningful
memories.

Its jaw slackens and its unquenchable thirst is satiated
only when it spies its pitiful prey
lying in a useless crumpled heap
on the ground in a numb nether world
bound buoyantly in a translucent tempest
devoid of all happiness
in the aftermath of its attack.

Revenge

Just a minute ago, we were so in love
Walking on air
hand in hand
Our minds, hearts and souls were one
It was the shit that poems are made of.

The next minute, my feet are dangling off the ground
Your hand clasped tightly around my throat.
I'm left gasping for air
body, mind and soul immersed in a war
I didn't ask to fight.
Like any good soldier I didn't leave you behind.
No matter how many times
You betrayed me
Not even when I was the victim of so called friendly fire.
Until that fateful day when you made me fight back and beg for my life and mercy.

So how did we get here?
Your eyes are filled with tears
Not for love lost, instead,
begging me for mercy, but
Mercy does not live here anymore.

My knife cuts through your tongue swiftly, lest you yell out in protest
proclaiming your abuse
by my hand.
I dangle your limp means of objection in front of your face mercilessly, then
toss it on the ground
Grinding it down with the heel of my shoe
It is useless, so full of lies, betrayal and abusive words.

I plunge my hand into your chest and pull out your black heart
I laugh and squeeze until your blood runs down my arm, staining it red, leaving a pool of coagulating at my feet
Shhh, don't look so horrified as I lick your blood off my arm, love.

Your life vitality beckons me to plunge my teeth into its crimson depths
It makes a delicious popping noise as I rip a chunk out and
Spit it in your face. I lick my lips pulling pieces of your pith out of my teeth.
Try not to look disgusted my love
It is common for warriors to eat the organs of their enemies.

Awakening

What has been seen cannot be unseen
seeds buried soul deep, push up through fertile flesh
emerging in rage filled
blood burgeoning pox
calculating cold fingers push them back in
better that they remain six feet under

Sickeningly sweet stench of bloated corpses rises from below
Dinner guests thank their host gagging down
the miasma permeated putrid meal.
Maggoty and rotting, they consciously consume
politely waiting to
voraciously vomit repulsive remains

Eyes once open cannot shut
peeled back like grapes, veins bulging,
watch, horror stricken, as
blood gushes through walls unchecked,
coagulating in slippery, sticky, scarlet
Puddles

Rising quickly, napkins symbolically raised,
Dabbing begins,
The deluge continues…
Nine months of crafty concealing gathers
around their feet
blood stained footprints left behind…

Now everyone will know

"Fiery Cradle"   CP

Fiery Cradle

If you have 3 children, you might as well have 10
So I'll send 3 down into the glen.
One two buckle their shoes
Wait till the neighbors hear the bad news
Three four, shut the barn door
After today seven wont need to be fed anymore
Five six, get a match stick,
hurry up, strike it quick.
Seven eight don't make the darlings wait
For their fiery fate.
Nine ten don't let them out again.
Oh no,
Here come the three up out of the glen.

Changeling

Weary wooden wagon wheels lazily wind down the path
Thump, bump, thump, bump
Dirty dust, rises up in swirly smoke
Dissipating like wispy ghosts
Crisp autumn air snaps, like the
Crack of a lightening fast whip
Giddyap! Giddyap!
On a road to nowhere, running away from mournful memories

Waaaa! Waaaa!
Urgent cries tug at mama's heart strings,
Horse's reins,
Woah! Woah!

Innocent cargo carelessly
Aborted
Loving arms swoop in
Scoop up, the gem
Hold the abandoned bundle tight
The night trudges on
slow as a funeral dirge

Surreal air, pregnant with an amaranth arsenic elixir
Slowly seeps its poison
Frothing, lathered equine hooves, churn mid air
Pawing at an invisible malleable malevolence
The babe taken from adoring arms,
rests on the buck board

Horses painfully plod on and on

Mammalian muscles strain, eyes bulge, bits bite into hot horse flesh
Yah yah!!!
Just one more step, then
Nothing

The orphaned babe once more, left behind
Garbage placed on the side of the road
The journey begins anew....

Evil cackles fill the air
Cold chills climb vertebrae like a xylophone dong
Glances backward reveal not the abandoned babe, but Lucifer
Dancing a jig in glee
Happy with the mischief he wrought

That Day

The deer carcass rolled in the ebb and flow of the waves
Making it look quite life like,
almost buoyant.
Closer inspection revealed,
Its bloated, decaying body, bloody and quite still,
portending what was to come later,

That day.

He and I walked past it, our eyes fixating, despite our best efforts, on
It's maggoty, half-eaten hind quarters and it's
Lifeless eyes. Life goes on though…
A neighbor arrived and covered the deer's rotted remains in a makeshift body bag,
the macabre vision temporarily stricken from our minds,.
we continued walking and exploring the beach for treasure,

That Day.

Fun and laughter filled the air,
Good memories were made in the hot summer sun.
Death jealous of our revelries, reminded us how fleeting life is,

That day.

The boy's lifeless body was taken from the lake,
police and relatives were called,
His body put in a bag like the deceased deer.
Lightening and thunder heralded the tragedy,

That night.

Rain poured down like a healing elixir,
In an attempt to cleanse our minds and the earth,
of the tragedies of,

That day.

"Red Canoe" CP

www.ingramcontent.com/pod-product-compliance
Lightning Source LLC
Chambersburg PA
CBHW042333150426

43194CB00001B/49